BENJAMIN FRANKLIN

BENJAMIN FRANKLIN

Peter and Connie Roop

For Father, who has shared his wit and wisdom over the years.

ACKNOWLEDGMENTS
The authors would especially like to thank Roy Goodman, Curator of Printed Materials, The American Philosophical Society, Philadelphia, for sharing his insights and enthusiasm about Benjamin Franklin.

Library of Congress Cataloging-in Publication Data
Roop, Connie.
Benjamin Franklin / Connie Roop and Peter Roop.
p. cm. — (In their own words)
Includes bibliographical references and index.
Summary: A biography of the noted statesman and inventor, featuring excerpts from his letters, pamphlets, essays, scientific papers, and autobiography.
1. Franklin, Benjamin, 1706-1790—Juvenile literature. 2. Statesmen—United States—Biography—Juvenile literature. 3. Inventors—United States—Biography—Juvenile literature. 4. Scientists—United States—Biography—Juvenile literature. 5. Printers—United States—Biographies—Juvenile literature. [1. Franklin, Benjamin, 1706-1790. 2. Statesmen. 3. Printers. 4. Scientists.] I. Roop Peter. II. Title. III. In their own words (Scholastic)
E302.6.F8 R73 2000
973.3'092—dc21   00-023183
ISBN 0-439-27179-7 (pob)
ISBN 0-439-15806-0 (pb)

10 9 8 7 6 5 4 3 2 1   01 02 03 04 05

Composition by Brad Walrod
Printed in the U.S.A.   23
First trade printing, September 2001

CONTENTS

INTRODUCTION

"DEAR SON: IMAGINING IT MAY BE agreeable to you to know the circumstances of my life, I sit down to write them for you."

Benjamin Franklin began his autobiography with these words for his son William. In it he told the story of his life in his own words. Always very busy, Franklin wrote his life's story in four stages over a period of thirty-three years. The last part was left unfinished when Franklin died at age eighty-four in 1790.

Benjamin Franklin led a most remarkable and full life. Through his letters, pamphlets, almanacs, autobiography, scientific papers, and essays, Franklin shares his eventful life.

In his words Benjamin Franklin revealed the wide range of his thinking. Through his letters he gave advice, discussed his scientific discoveries, and asked questions. In his printed work he shared humor and informed people. His ideas helped create the United States of America. His wise words shaped the thinking of generations of Americans and Europeans.

Benjamin Franklin loved the written word. He learned to read at an early age. "I do not remember when I could not read," he wrote. He became a master printer and writer. Altogether, Franklin's collected writings could fill fifty books.

During his lifetime, Ben saw America change in many ways. Massachusetts was no longer a colony of England. It became one of the thirteen states of the young United States. Philadelphia replaced Boston as the most important city in America. The American Revolution was fought and won. A unique government was created under a constitution. Lightning wasn't a terrifying mystery anymore. It was known to be electricity. Libraries, hospitals, fire

Through his words Benjamin Franklin became one of the most important men of the eighteenth century. He is remembered as an inventor, a scientist, a diplomat, an author, and a printer.

departments, and universities were founded. Ben Franklin played an important role in each of these events.

Franklin's autobiography and his other writings are called primary sources. A primary source is a first-hand account of an event. Primary sources are eyewitness versions of events a person saw or in which he or she participated. Speeches, letters, diaries, government documents, and autobiographies are primary sources.

Christopher Columbus's journal is a primary source. So is Martin Luther King Jr.'s "I Have A Dream" speech. A video you make of a parade or party is another primary source.

Reading primary sources is the next best thing to talking with the person about whom you are learning. Through his or her own words, you see the world through that person's eyes.

Secondary sources, such as encyclopedias, are another way to learn about a person or an event. A secondary source is a description of an event written by someone who was not actually there. A biography of George Washington is a secondary source. This book is a secondary source.

Ben Franklin's autobiography, letters, and writings were used as primary sources to write this book. Biographies of Franklin and materials found during a visit to Philadelphia were secondary sources.

By reading Franklin's words you can sense the thrill of scientific discovery. You can smile at the humor of people who lived long ago. You can witness the birth of the United States and the creation of our Constitution. You can see what one person can do to better the lives of all people.

Now, through many of his own words, meet Benjamin Franklin.

CHILD

JANUARY 17, 1706 DAWNED COLD IN Boston, Massachusetts Colony. The sign outside of Josiah Franklin's home and shop swung in the chilly breeze. The Franklin house on Milk Street was crowded. This day a new voice was added to the chorus: Benjamin Franklin's.

"I was the youngest son, and the youngest child but two, and was born in Boston, New England," Franklin wrote in his autobiography. Ben was the fifteenth of the seventeen Franklin children. Altogether there were seven Franklin daughters and ten Franklin sons. Imagine the hustle and bustle of the Franklin home!

When Ben was born, Boston was the largest and most important city in the English colonies.

Yet its population was only about 12,000. Today, over half a million people live in Boston.

Ben's father, Josiah Franklin, was a candle-maker and soap-maker. Josiah had been born in England in 1657. He had come to America to make a better life for himself and his growing family.

"Josiah, my father, married young and carried his wife with three children to New England," Ben wrote. His English ancestors had been blacksmiths, farmers, and cloth dyers. Ben Franklin admired his English family.

Ben wrote this about his father: "He had a most excellent constitution of body, was of middle stature, but well set, and very strong." Josiah was also talented. "He...could draw prettily, was a little skilled in music. He was very handy in the use of other trademen's tools." What Ben appreciated most, however, was his father's "sound understanding and solid judgment," in both private and public affairs.

Josiah Franklin's first wife Anne died six years after the couple reached America. He struggled to

Josiah Franklin and his family moved into this house on Milk Street in Boston in 1685.

care for his five children and build his business. A short time after Anne's death, he married Abiah Folger.

Abiah was a twenty-two-year-old woman from Nantucket, Massachusetts Colony. As Ben said, "My mother, the second wife, was Abiah Folger, daughter of Peter Folger, one of the first settlers of New England." From both his parents, young Ben gained attributes that proved valuable all his life.

When the Milk Street house grew too crowded, the family moved. The Franklins now lived in a bigger home. They lived upstairs. Below was Mr. Franklin's soap and candle shop.

Ben Franklin wrote little about his childhood. One incident he related taught him the value of money. This happened when he was seven years old.

"My friends, on a holiday, filled my pockets with coppers [coins]. I went directly to a shop where they sold toys for children. Being charmed with the sound of a whistle . . . I gave all my money for one. I then came home and went whistling all over the

A blue ball bearing the date 1698 hung outside Josiah Franklin's shop. It served as his business sign.

house, much pleased with my whistle, but disturbing all the family."

Ben was proud of himself. He thought he had paid a fair price for the whistle. But his family teased him. They said it wasn't such a good deal after all. "My brothers and sisters and cousins...told me I had given four times as much for it as it was worth."

Ben's feelings were hurt and he cried. Later, he wrote a saying about the lesson he learned, "Save and have."

Ben was an outgoing boy and he had many friends. "I was generally a leader among the boys, and sometimes led them into scrapes."

One day Ben and his friends were fishing for minnows at the edge of a marsh. Their feet had churned the earth into mud. Ben had an idea. If they built a wharf, they could fish from it. It would keep their feet clean and dry. Ben decided he would take stones from a nearby construction site. When the workers had gone home, Ben brought his friends to the site.

"I showed my comrades a large heap of stones . . . which would very well suit our purpose." That night, Ben and his friends took the heavy stones and "built our little wharf."

Trouble loomed. The next morning the workmen were surprised to find their stones missing. "We were discovered and complained of."

Ben's father made him tear down the wharf and return the stones. Ben said, "Though I pleaded the usefulness of the work, [my father] convinced me nothing was useful which was not honest."

Ben was also a leader when it came to swimming and boating. "Living near the water, I was much in and about it, learning early to swim well and to manage boats." When in a boat or canoe with other boys, Ben was in charge.

Swimming was one of Ben's greatest skills. Frequently, he would dive into water, especially when the weather was hot. He taught his friends how to swim.

One day Ben thought of a way to swim faster. He knew ducks had webbed feet to help them swim better. He thought that if his hands and feet were webbed, he could swim faster. So Ben made paddles for his hands to pull him through the water. He tied paddles to his feet so he could kick harder. His idea worked wonderfully. Now he could swim farther and faster than any of his friends!

Another day while swimming he had a new idea. What would happen if he flew a kite while he was in the water? He wondered if the kite would pull him across the pond.

Ben flew his kite high in the sky. Floating on his back, he held the kite string. He was thrilled to be towed across the pond with no effort at all! His friends quickly joined him in this new sport.

Life was not all play for Ben. His parents knew how clever he was. So, at age eight, he was sent to school. In the early 1700s, few children went to school. But Ben's father wanted him to be a minister when he grew up. To be a minister, Ben had to go to grammar school and learn Latin.

Ben went to a grammar school with one hundred boys. He studied hard and became the best in his class. "I had risen gradually from the middle of the class to be the head of it." He did so well he even skipped a grade.

Grammar school was expensive. After one year Josiah could no longer afford to send Ben there. Ben would not be a minister. Instead Ben started at a less

Ben Franklin loved to read and learn throughout his life. He wrote, "The doors to wisdom are never shut."

expensive school for writing and arithmetic. Josiah wanted Ben to have those skills so he could help with the family business. Ben did well with writing, "but I failed in the arithmetic, and made no progress in it."

Soon, Josiah thought Ben had learned enough at school. Now he needed to work. With so many mouths to feed and bodies to clothe, Josiah Franklin had to make his children work. "My elder brothers were all put to apprentices to different trades," Ben wrote.

"At ten years old I was taken home to assist my father in his business. I was employed cutting wick for the candles, filling the dipping mold and the molds for cast candles, attending the shop, going on errands."

Ben did not like working in the candle shop. He didn't mind working twelve hours a day, six days a week. But the work was boring. The shop smelled bad because the candles and soap were made from animal fat. The shop was hot from the kettles that heated the fat so it could be poured into molds.

"I disliked the trade," Ben wrote. He wanted to be a sailor. "I had a strong inclination for the sea, but my father declared against it." One of Ben's older brothers disobeyed Josiah and became a sailor. Josiah was afraid that Ben might run away to be a sailor, too. He decided Ben must find a trade he liked and become an apprentice.

In early America, being an apprentice was the way a boy learned the skills of a trade. A boy would be an apprentice to a blacksmith, bricklayer, carpenter, tailor, printer, or other tradesman. Then he could earn a living as an adult.

To find the right apprenticeship for his son, Josiah took Ben around Boston. They watched many different tradesmen and craftsmen at work. Ben was delighted. Always curious, he enjoyed watching men working with their tools at their trades.

"It has ever been a pleasure to me to see good workmen handle their tools; and it has been useful to me, having learnt so much by it as to be able to do little jobs myself in my house . . . and to construct little machines for my experiments."

However, Ben did not like the trades he saw. Then Josiah remembered Ben's love of words. Ben recalled, "From a child I was fond of reading, and all the little money that came into my hands was ever laid out in books." Ben read the books he bought and then sold them to get new ones. He also read the Bible and other religious books in his father's small library.

Maybe becoming a printer was just the trade for Ben, Josiah thought. Ben could be an apprentice to his older brother James in his printing shop. This time Josiah chose well.

APPRENTICE

IN 1717, JAMES FRANKLIN HAD SET UP his printing business in Boston. Ben visited his brother's shop. He liked printing much better than soap-making. But sometimes he still dreamed of a life at sea.

Josiah was fearful Ben would be a sailor. He pressured Ben to agree to be a printer's apprentice. At first Ben refused. But finally, he gave in to his father's demands.

"I stood out some time, but at last was persuaded, and signed the [agreement] when I was but twelve years old. I was to serve as an apprentice till I was twenty-one years of age."

When Ben signed the papers, he agreed to do

whatever work James ordered: sweep the floor, set type, make ink, sell goods, greet customers, and operate the printing press. In return, James would provide Ben with room and board. He would teach him the printing business. Ben would not get paid for his work until his last year. For eight years he would work for only food, lodging, and training.

Ben took to printing as eagerly as he had to swimming. He wrote, "In a little time I [learned] the business, and became a useful hand to my brother." In Ben's time there were no radios and televisions. Newspapers, pamphlets, and posters were the way news was shared and ideas were discussed. So people who printed them were very important.

Ben was good with words. He easily mastered the printer's skills. He set the type quickly and accurately. Each lead letter had to be individually selected and placed in a line from right to left. When an entire page was ready, it was set in the press. Then it was covered with ink, and the heavy press handle was turned. The white paper was

Ben (center) quickly became skilled at the printing press. After a sheet of paper was printed, he would hang it to dry.

pressed against the letters and the words were printed on the page.

A printing shop was a busy and noisy place. Customers were served, letters set, and pages were printed. Ben enjoyed the way words and ideas flowed there.

Ben made friends with the apprentices of booksellers. From them, he could borrow more books. He wrote, "I now had access to better books.

Often I sat in my room reading the greatest part of the night." An early riser, he would return a book "early in the morning, lest it should be missed."

One friend, Matthew Adams, invited Ben to use his personal library. In those days most books were imported from England. They were expensive. Only a few wealthy people had many books. Being able to borrow them regularly from Matthew pleased Ben. He could read all he wanted and not have to spend a penny. Ben read widely: science, religion, novels, and essays. He enjoyed poetry so much that he tried writing poems.

"I now took a fancy to poetry, and made some little pieces," Ben once wrote. James thought he could profit from Ben's skill with words so he encouraged him. Ben printed the poems and walked around Boston selling them.

Josiah Franklin did not like this. "My father discouraged me," Ben recalled. "So I escaped being a poet, most probably a very bad one."

Yet Ben enjoyed writing. He worked hard to improve this skill. How did Ben find time for extra

Ben sold his poems on the streets of Boston. His father did not want Ben to write poetry. He told him that poets "were always beggars."

study? He stayed up late writing and reading. He got up early to do the same. On Sundays he missed church so he could be alone in the printing shop.

Throughout his life Benjamin Franklin looked for ways to improve himself. When he was sixteen, Ben decided not to eat meat. Instead he ate potatoes, rice, bread, water, hasty pudding, vegetables, and raisins. He felt this would make him healthier.

James paid for his apprentices to eat at a nearby house. Ben knew his meals cost very little. Meat was more expensive than vegetables.

Ben suggested that James give him half of what he normally paid for Ben's meals. He would then feed himself. James, thinking he had gotten the best of his brother, readily agreed.

As it turned out, Ben had made a good deal. He was able to feed himself very cheaply. He did not need to spend all of James's money on food. The leftover money was used for books. Also, Ben enjoyed the times when the other workers went out to eat. He was able to eat and read in the quiet printing shop.

Ben made great progress in his studies. He even mastered arithmetic, which he had failed in school. The lesson of small meals stayed with Ben all his life. As an adult he wrote, "Eat to live, and not live to eat."

The wooden printing press Ben Franklin used while he was a printer's apprentice in Boston

In 1721, James Franklin started his own newspaper. At that time there was one local paper, the *Boston News-Letter*. James named his paper *The New England Courant*. James filled his paper with articles about New England events and people. Ben's job was to print and sell the newspapers.

Some of James's friends wrote amusing pieces for the paper. Ben decided to try such writing, too. As the master of the shop, James sometimes bullied Ben. Ben knew that James would not publish his stories.

So Ben pretended to be Silence Dogood, a widow with funny opinions and observations. He disguised his handwriting so James would not know he was Silence Dogood. At night Ben slipped his stories under the printing house door.

James was delighted at the unknown author's wit. He eagerly published Silence Dogood. The newspaper's readers enjoyed "her" as well. Ben was excited by his success. He wrote fourteen Silence Dogood pieces.

But Ben eventually grew tired of writing secretly. He wanted James to know he had written the

Dogood stories. So Ben revealed Silence Dogood's true identity to James. Instead of being pleased, James was angry that Ben had tricked him.

Ben was tired of his brother's harsh actions. He wanted to end his apprenticeship. Sadly, there was nothing to be done.

Then James got into trouble. He printed a story that upset members of the Massachusetts Assembly. The Assembly helped to govern the colony. They ordered that, "James Franklin should no longer print the paper called *The New England Courant.*"

Because he could no longer print the paper, James decided to print the paper under Ben's name. Ben agreed. But he also made James sign a new apprenticeship agreement. James, eager to publish, agreed to Ben's terms.

But Ben was tired of working for James. He made up his mind to leave. James did not like this so he told other printers in Boston not to give Ben a job.

Frustrated, Ben made a decision that changed his life. He would run away. "So I sold some of my books to raise a little money, was taken aboard [a ship] privately, and as we had a fair wind, in three days I found myself in New York, nearly 300 miles from home, a boy of but 17...with very little money in my pocket."

RUNAWAY

BEN PICKED NEW YORK BECAUSE IT was the closest city to Boston that had a newspaper. He asked a printer named William Bradford for a job. Bradford told Ben that he had just hired someone. He suggested that Ben go to Philadelphia instead. His son Andrew might need help in his printing shop. Ben agreed.

Ben reached Philadelphia early on a Sunday morning. Here is Ben's description of his arrival in the city.

"I was in my working dress. I was dirty from my journey and my pockets were stuffed out with shirts and stockings. I knew no soul nor where to look for lodging. Fatigued with walking, rowing, and want of sleep, I was very hungry."

Ben decided to spend his last coins for bread. He went to a baker's shop. "He gave me three great puffy rolls. I was surprised at the quantity but took it, and having no room in my pockets, walked off with a roll under each arm and eating the other."

Dirty and tired, with clothes spilling from his pockets, Ben strolled up Market Street. He heard a laugh. A young woman was staring at him and giggling. "She saw me, and thought I made—as I certainly did—a most awkward, ridiculous appearance."

The girl was Deborah Read. One day she and Ben would marry.

Ben marched on, nibbling a roll. When he was full, he generously gave the remaining bread to a hungry woman and her child.

Philadelphia was a young city when Ben arrived in 1723. It had been founded in 1681. Fewer than 10,000 people lived there. By the time of the American Revolution in 1775, Philadelphia had grown to be the most important city in America.

Deborah Read looks on as Ben Franklin walks up Market Street in Philadelphia with bread under each arm.

The only larger city in the British empire was London.

On his second day in town, Ben went to find work at Andrew Bradford's printing shop. But Mr. Bradford had no openings. He told Ben to ask Samuel Keimer, a fellow printer, if he needed help.

Keimer asked Ben questions, had him set some type, and then hired him. Keimer did not have a place for Ben to stay. He arranged for Ben to live with Mr. Read. He was the father of the girl who had so recently laughed at Ben! "I made rather a more respectable appearance in the eyes of Miss Read than I had done when she first happened to see me eating my roll in the street," Ben wrote.

Ben continued to work hard and save money. Because of his cheerfulness and humor, Ben soon made friends among the other workers.

Ben came to the attention of Sir William Keith, governor of Pennsylvania. Sir William met Ben and liked him. The governor, "made me many compliments," Ben wrote.

Sir William suggested that Ben set up his own printing shop. He promised Ben the official printing business of Pennsylvania. Ben was excited by this idea. He would be his own boss and have his own printing business.

Ben needed money to open his own shop. He had

none. So, with a letter from Sir William, Ben sailed to Boston to ask for his father's help.

No one had heard from Ben in seven months. His return was a pleasure. "My unexpected appearance surpris'd the family; all were, however, very glad to see me, and made me welcome, except my brother [James]."

Ben visited James at his printing shop. He wanted to get along better with his brother. James received him coldly. Ben was willing to forgive his brother's meanness to him. He had hoped "we might live for the future as brothers." James thought otherwise. Ben's apprentice friends, however, were delighted to hear his adventures. Ben proudly displayed his watch, a rare thing for a young man to own. Ben then gave his friends money to entertain themselves.

This gift angered James. "He said I had insulted him in such a manner before his people that he could never forget or forgive it," Ben wrote.

Josiah questioned Ben about Sir William and his printing proposal. Ben's father was surprised Sir

Sir William Keith visits Ben in the printing shop where he worked.

William put so much faith in such a young man. After thinking about the idea, Josiah wrote to Sir William. He said he would not give Ben the money now. Ben was too young and inexperienced. If by age twenty-one Ben had proved himself capable of running his own business, Josiah would help then.

Ben returned to Philadelphia without the money, but with his father's blessing.

Sir William decided to establish Ben in the printing business himself. He told Ben to sail to London to buy a press and type. When he returned, he could open his own shop. Sir William promised

Ben a letter of credit. Ben could use it to buy what he needed when he reached London. Ben would be given the letter there.

While he waited for a ship that would cross the Atlantic, Ben courted Deborah Read. Deborah's mother agreed to their marriage. But Ben and Deborah had to wait until Ben came home from London. Excited about his future, Ben set sail on November 5, 1724.

However, Ben had a disappointing surprise when he arrived in London. Sir William had never written the letter! Now Ben had no money to buy the printing press or to return home.

Ben Franklin arrived in London on Christmas Eve, 1724. He was penniless and without a job.

LONDONER

WITH HIS SKILLS, PERSONALITY, and determination, Ben did well in London. First, he worked at Palmer's Printing House and then at James Watt's printing shop.

Lifting and setting heavy pages of lead type had made Ben strong. He was hardworking and friendly. He quickly became popular with his fellow printers. Ben drank only water and ate sparingly, much to the amusement of his new companions. He swam in the river Thames, showing off his swimming skills. He taught his friends how to swim, too.

Ben loved the sights, sounds, and scenes of London. He enjoyed going to the theater and

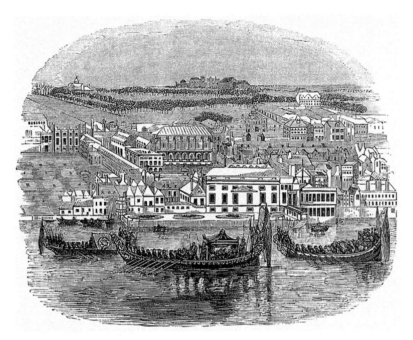

Eighteenth-century London was busy and crowded. By 1800, its population would grow to one million people. It was the largest city in the world.

visiting bookshops. He spent long hours conversing with his friends.

While in London, Ben kept in touch with Thomas Denham. Mr. Denham was a Philadelphia merchant Ben met on the voyage to London. They often talked and ate together. Denham was returning to Philadelphia to open a store. He asked Ben to join him and become his clerk. He would pay Ben's way home. A homesick Ben agreed.

In July 1726, Benjamin Franklin returned to America. The ocean voyage was long, but Ben enjoyed himself. He read and wrote in his journal. He observed dolphins, sharks, and flying fish. He studied the ocean currents and weather. When the ship sailed slowly, he swam alongside it to bathe.

After three months at sea, the ship reached Philadelphia on October 11, 1726.

Mr. Denham opened his store and Ben went to work. In February 1727, both Ben and Mr. Denham became very ill. Mr. Denham died and "left me once more in the wild world."

Ben was twenty-one and on his own again.

PRINTER

BEN SWALLOWED HIS PRIDE. HE returned to Samuel Keimer and humbly asked for a job. Keimer was pleased to see him. He made Ben the manager of his printing shop. Ben would teach Keimer's printers how to do better work.

Ben trained Keimer's young apprentices. He made type and ink. He soon had the printing shop in good order and making a profit. Then, when everything was running well, Keimer cut Ben's wages. They argued and Ben quit.

When Ben left Keimer's shop, his fellow printer Hugh Meredith left with him. Hugh's father had money to invest. He used it to help Hugh and Ben open their own printing business.

Mr. Meredith felt that with Ben's skills and energy, the print shop would succeed. He also hoped the hard work would keep Hugh out of trouble.

Ben threw himself into the new business. He woke early and worked late. "He who riseth late, must trot all day," he said. He dressed plainly and rarely took time off for any entertainment except reading. To make a good appearance in public, Ben bought paper and wheeled it to the shop himself. He wanted others to see how hard he worked.

In 1729, Ben decided Philadelphia needed a second newspaper. Samuel Keimer heard of Ben's idea. He was jealous. So he quickly began a paper of his own called *The Pennsylvania Gazette*. Ben was upset that Keimer started a paper first. But instead of causing trouble, he wrote for the rival paper *The Mercury*. *The Mercury* did well while sales of *The Pennsylvania Gazette* fell. In less than a year Keimer gave up the struggle. He sold his newspaper to Ben and moved away. Now Franklin and Meredith were publishers of *The Pennsylvania Gazette*.

Hugh Meredith, however, was not much help to

Numb. XL.

THE
Pennſylvania GAZETTE.

Containing the freſheſt Advices Foreign and Domeſtick.

From Thurſday, September 25. to Thurſday, October 2. 1729.

THE Pennſylvania Gazette *being now to be carry'd on by other Hands, the Reader may expect ſome Account of the Method we deſign to proceed in.*

Upon a View of Chambers's *great Dictionaries, from whence were taken the Materials of the* Univerſal Inſtructor *in all Arts and Sciences, which uſually made the Firſt Part of this Paper, we find that beſides their containing many Things abſtruſe or inſignificant to us, it will probably be fifty Years before the Whole can be gone thro' in this Manner of Publication. There are likewiſe in thoſe Books continual References from Things under one Letter of the Alphabet to thoſe under another, which relate to the ſame Subject, and are neceſſary to explain and compleat it; theſe taken in their Turn may perhaps be Ten Years diſtant; and ſince it is likely that they who deſire to acquaint themſelves with any particular Art or Science, would gladly have the whole before them in a much leſs Time, we believe our Readers will not think ſuch a Method of communicating Knowledge to be a proper One.*

However, tho' we do not intend to continue the Publication of thoſe Dictionaries in a regular Alphabetical Method, as has hitherto been done; yet as ſeveral Things exhibited from them in the Courſe of theſe Papers, have been entertaining to ſuch of the Curious, who never had and cannot have the Advantage of good Libraries; and as there are many Things ſtill behind, which being in this Manner made generally known, may perhaps become of conſiderable Uſe, by giving ſuch Hints to the excellent natural Genius's of our Country, as may contribute either to the Improvement of our preſent Manufactures, or towards the Invention of new Ones; we propoſe from Time to Time to communicate ſuch Particular

There are many who have long deſired to ſee a good News-Paper in Pennſylvania, *and we hope thoſe Gentlemen who are able, will contribute towards the making This ſuch. We ask Aſſiſtance, becauſe we are fully ſenſible, that to publiſh a good News-Paper is not ſo eaſy an Undertaking as many People imagine it to be. The Author of a Gazette (in the Opinion of the Learned) ought to be qualified with an extenſive Acquaintance with Languages, a great Eaſineſs and Command of Writing and Relating Things cleanly and intelligibly, and in few Words; he ſhould be able to ſpeak of War both by Land and Sea; be well acquainted with Geography, with the Hiſtory of the Time, with the ſeveral Intereſts of Princes and States, the Secrets of Courts, and the Manners and Cuſtoms of all Nations. Men thus accompliſh'd are very rare in this remote Part of the World; and it would be well if the Writer of theſe Papers could make up among his Friends what is wanting in himſelf.*

Upon the Whole, we may aſſure the Publick, that as far as the Encouragement we meet with will enable us, no Care and Pains ſhall be omitted, that may make the Pennſylvania Gazette *as agreeable and uſeful an Entertainment as the Nature of the Thing will allow.*

The Following is the laſt Meſſage ſent by his Excellency Governour *Burnet*, to the Houſe of Repreſentatives in *Boſton*.

Gentlemen of the Houſe of Repreſentatives,

IT is not with ſo vain a Hope as to convince you, that I take the Trouble to anſwer your Meſſages, but, if poſſible, to open the Eyes of the deluded People whom you repreſent, and whom you are at ſo much Pains to keep

This issue of The Pennsylvania Gazette *promises that the newspaper will be "as agreeable and useful an Entertainment as the Nature of the Thing will allow."*

Ben. So they arranged for Meredith to sell his share of the business to Ben. The deal was a friendly one. Meredith did not enjoy the hard work needed to make the business successful.

In 1729, at twenty-three years of age, Ben was running his own business. But he felt he could not make a good living just printing books, newspapers, and pamphlets. So Ben also sold paper, ink, and his father's soap. His customers could buy coffee, lottery tickets, maps, quill pens, and tea. He also became the only bookseller in Philadelphia. Ben advertised his goods in his newspaper, which brought more customers into his shop.

Ben also advertised slaves for sale. Slaves were bought and sold throughout the colonies at this time. Franklin himself sometimes owned slaves. Later in his life, Ben became a powerful voice for freedom. He spoke out against slavery. In 1787, he founded and became president of The Pennsylvania Society for Promoting the Abolition of Slavery. This was the first group to work to end slavery in America.

Throughout his life, Ben liked to learn. He began

meeting with eleven young men who also enjoyed learning. With them, he formed a club called "The Junto." Ben called it "a club for mutual improvement." He quickly became the leader of the Junto.

The Junto met on Friday evenings to discuss ideas and solve problems. They talked about books and science. They made plans to help other young tradesmen similar to themselves.

The Junto members also liked to read. Ben suggested that they pool their books to create a library. This way they could share the expense of buying books. Ben felt it would be as if they all owned a large library.

This library lasted a year. Then Ben had another idea. Why not invite more people to form a bigger library? Each person would pay money to join. The money would be used to buy books. Then each person could borrow books. Fifty people signed up. An order for books was sent to London. In October 1731, the books arrived in Philadelphia. There were novels, essays, dictionaries, and science books.

Ben (standing at center) at the opening of Philadelphia's first subscription library

This library became the first public library in America. Ben's idea was copied in other American colonies. This library still exists as the Free Library of Philadelphia. At first, it had only a few books. Today the Free Library has millions of them.

While Ben was away in London, he had neglected Deborah Read. When he returned, he proposed again to Deborah. She accepted and they were married on September 1, 1730. Together Ben and Deborah raised three children: William, Francis, and Sally. Ben adored his children and wished he had more.

Tragedy struck when Francis died at age four from smallpox. Ben loved this lively little boy who was so much like himself. For the rest of his life Ben carried a picture of his "Franky" with him whenever he traveled. Thirty-six years after Franky's death Ben wrote, "To this day I cannot think of [Franky] without a sigh."

Deborah was a good wife, mother, and business partner. Like Ben, she did not hide from hard work. She helped Ben at home and in his shop. Later, when he went to Europe, she watched over his business. She supervised the building of their house.

Just twenty-four years old, the runaway from Boston was now happily married and a respected businessman.

Ben began adding to his printing business. In the 1700s, books were scarce and expensive. Many people learned to read from either the Bible or an almanac. Almanacs were small, cheap publications.

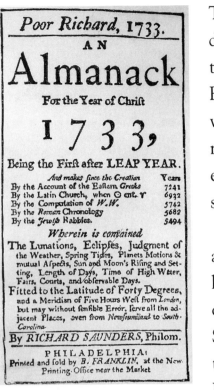

A page from the first edition of Poor Richard's Almanack, *which was published in December 1732.*

They contained calendars, weather predictions, and proverbs. Readers enjoyed their witty sayings, jokes, recipes, and whatever else the publisher could squeeze in.

Ben decided to write and print an almanac himself. He created a character as he did with Silence Dogood. This time his "voice" was Richard Saunders, a poor man with a proud wife. Ben nicknamed his character Poor Richard. From Poor Richard's pen came the funny and very successful *Poor Richard's Almanack.* (Almanac was spelled with a "k" in Franklin's time.)

Poor Richard made Ben rich. As his publisher,

Ben was well-known throughout the colonies and Europe. Ben wrote and published *Poor Richard's Almanack* from 1732 (the same year George Washington was born) until 1758. *Poor Richard's Almanack* was a bestseller throughout the colonies. Only the Bible sold more copies.

Poor Richard's sayings included, "Early to bed, early to rise, makes a man healthy, wealthy, and wise." "Fish and visitors stink after three days." "Haste makes waste." "Lost time is never found again." "Little strokes fell great oaks."

With his business a success, Ben wanted to make Philadelphia a safer and more pleasant place to live. First, he turned his attention to paving the streets. At the time, Philadelphia's streets were wide and straight. But none were paved. When it was dry, dust covered people and buildings. When it rained, the streets became muddy. Mud was tracked into homes and shops.

Tired of the messy streets, Ben wanted to pave them with cobblestones. He made his plans. He wrote a letter for *The Pennsylvania Gazette* pointing out the problem. He suggested that the streets be paved with stones. He talked about his idea with his friends and neighbors. After he had spread his idea around, he had a busy street near the market paved. People were extremely pleased.

Ben went further. He found a man who would sweep the paved street. Each homeowner along the street paid a small fee for this service. Before long other people wanted their streets paved and swept. Then Ben took his plan to the city government. They agreed to tax people to pave all the streets and have them cleaned. They even added streetlights!

Ben never liked waste. Fire was extremely wasteful and dangerous. Much of Philadelphia was made of wood and brick. Fire could destroy these buildings quickly. So, Ben set out to form a fire department. First, he discussed his idea with the Junto. They thought it was an excellent plan and agreed to help Ben.

But Ben had to convince other Philadelphians of the value of a fire department. To plant the idea, he wrote a letter for his newspaper. He asked people to be careful when carrying coals from one fireplace to another. This, he thought, would get folks thinking about fire prevention.

Then he explained how Boston had fire clubs. Their job was to put out fires and save lives and property. These firemen practiced regularly to improve their skills. Ben explained that, since Boston had these fire clubs, there had not been any major fires. "I wish there never may be any here," he wrote.

The people of Philadelphia agreed with Ben's suggestion. Thirty volunteers joined Ben to form the Union Fire Company in 1736. Each volunteer had a leather bucket for carrying water. Everyone had a strong basket to rescue things from burning buildings. The group met once a month to talk about how to put out fires. They also practiced.

Soon other fire companies were formed. The fire companies bought fire engines, ladders, and hoses. Before long, most of Philadelphia was protected.

Ben then turned his attention to protecting people from theft. At the time, most homes were protected by night watchmen. Sometimes these men failed to walk their rounds. They got distracted by other activities. Ben felt that the watchmen needed to be better organized. He also believed the watchmen should be carefully selected and better paid.

Ben discussed his ideas with the Junto. Word spread to other clubs. This improvement took longer to complete than organizing the fire companies. But Philadelphia did create its own police force, one of the first in the country.

Even as a boy Ben had been curious. He was interested in the world around him. He observed plants and animals. He chased tornadoes on horseback. He studied storms. He collected rocks.

Wishing to share his knowledge and increase it, Ben had another idea. Why not form a society to spread scientific knowledge? This group would have members throughout the thirteen colonies, not just in Philadelphia. The members would share what they knew about science, plants, animals, and geography. They would write letters discussing weather, inventions, and mathematics. They would help make maps and do experiments.

In 1744, Ben Franklin founded the American Philosophical Society. Ten members joined. Ben was its first president. When he retired, Thomas Jefferson became president of the society. Today the American Philosophical Society still supports scientific knowledge in America and around the world.

Not all of the city improvements were Ben's ideas. Dr. Thomas Bond, a friend and member of the Junto, suggested a hospital. There were no hospitals anywhere in America at the time. Ben agreed to help. Once again, he wrote letters for his newspaper. He convinced people that a hospital was necessary. He suggested ways to raise money. Before long, Philadelphia had its first hospital.

Always a lover of learning, Ben felt Philadelphia needed a college. There were only three colleges in the colonies at the time. Again, he shared his idea with the Junto. Working tirelessly, he convinced others to support a college. Within a year the college opened. Today that college is the University of Pennsylvania.

Ben began a school for boys and girls. He remembered how he could not attend school for long because his family had no money to spare. So Ben arranged for poor children to go to his school for free.

During this time Ben's curiosity turned to inventions. He realized how much heat was wasted in open fireplaces. He invented the Franklin stove, which saved wood and heated rooms better.

Each time Ben invented something he refused to take out a patent and profit from it. He said, "As we enjoy great advantages from the inventions of others, we should be glad of an opportunity to serve others by an invention of ours: and this we should do freely and generously."

With his businesses doing so well, Ben decided to retire from daily work in 1748 at age forty-two. He wanted to have time to "read, study, and make

The Franklin stove, invented around 1740, was used in American homes for more than 200 years.

experiments and converse . . . on such points as may produce something for the common benefits of mankind."

Little did he know the impact this decision would have, not only on himself, but the world.

SCIENTIST

IN 1746, BENJAMIN FRANKLIN HAD become interested in electricity. Now that he was retired, Ben devoted himself to understanding electricity better. "I never was before engaged in any study that so totally engrossed my attention and my time," he wrote.

At this time, electricity was played with for entertainment. Tricks were performed. Sparks were passed through people or pulled from someone's ear. Objects were made to sparkle.

Ben sensed there was more to electricity than just tricks. He bought his own electrical equipment and began experimenting. People dropped in to see his experiments. His house on

Market Street was "continually full with people who came by to see these new wonders."

Using other scientists' ideas, Ben added his own insights. He realized that electricity flows from one object to another. He created words to describe electricity that we still use: positive and negative, charge, battery, electrician, and electrify.

Ben thought that electricity and lightning were alike. Maybe they were the same thing. He wrote, "The electrical fluid is attracted by points. We do not know whether this property is in lightning."

Because he did not know, Ben decided to find out. "Let the experiment be made," he said.

Ben thought people should attach a pointed rod to their homes and barns. He guessed that these lightning rods would protect them from lightning strikes. The rods would draw the electrical charge out of the clouds and down into the ground. Lightning would hit the rod, not the home. But it remained just an idea until he could prove it.

Ben shared his knowledge of electricity with friends and other scientists. He wrote letters. He published pamphlets describing his discoveries and ideas. In March 1752, the French scientist D'Alibard used Franklin's idea. He placed a pointed rod in the ground before a storm rumbled in. Lightning struck the rod with an explosive crack. Franklin was right!

Ben used this machine to create electricity for some of his experiments.

Ben still wanted to prove that lightning was electricity. He knew lightning happened during thunderstorms. It was then he had the idea for which he is probably most famous. He would fly a kite during a thunderstorm! If the kite went high enough, he thought, it would attract an electrical charge from the clouds. The charge would flow down the kite string. Then he would feel the charge!

But this would only happen if lightning was indeed electricity.

Ben did not understand how dangerous this experiment was. He should have known. Two years before, in 1750, he had decided to show the power of electricity. He had tried to kill a turkey for dinner with electricity from his batteries. Instead, he almost killed himself. "I took the whole [charge] through my own arms and body. I felt a blow throughout my whole body from head to foot." Dazed from the shock, Ben took hours to recover. "I am ashamed to have been guilty of so notorious a blunder," he wrote.

In September 1752, Ben decided to try his kite experiment. With his son William (who was twenty-one years old at the time) Ben built a kite from a silk handkerchief. He attached a string to the kite to bring the lightning down toward the earth. He knew that electricity charged metal so he hung a key close to his hand. Ben guessed that if lightning were electricity, it would flow down the string. He would then feel it in the key.

Ben and William flew the kite in a storm. For a

Ben and William Franklin fly a kite in a thunderstorm. They used a Leyden jar (bottom left) to collect an electrical charge that Ben could experiment with later.

long time, however, nothing happened. Then Ben saw loose threads on the string stand up. Electricity was present! He held his knuckle out toward the key. A brilliant spark leaped from the key to his finger. Ben knew he had proved that lightning was indeed electricity.

Imagine how wonderful Ben must have felt at

that moment. He was also incredibly lucky. The wet string had not conducted a large electrical charge to his hand. If it had, he might have been killed.

Up until that time, many people thought lightning was sent by God. They believed wrongdoers were being punished when lightning struck their homes. But Franklin had shown that lightning was a part of nature.

Ben convinced people to protect their buildings from lightning with lightning rods. He would be the first to protect his home. Soon others set up lightning rods. Today lightning rods are used throughout the world.

Franklin refused to take out a patent on his lightning rod. As usual, he wished all of mankind to benefit from his discovery.

Ben's fame as the tamer of lightning spread quickly in America and Europe. The following year Harvard College and Yale College honored Ben with degrees. In November 1753, the Royal Society, England's most famous scientific organization, awarded Ben its highest honor. He was given the society's Copley gold medal for "his curious experiments and observations on electricity."

Ben now worked to improve the colonial postal system. In 1753, Ben was appointed Deputy Postmaster General. At the time, the mail system was poorly managed. Ben wanted to make mail delivery more reliable. He wrote instructions for local postmasters. He developed schedules for faster, more frequent postal delivery service.

Making these improvements meant traveling to every colony. Ben selected the best mail routes. He hired capable men to carry the mail. To measure distances accurately, Franklin invented the odometer. He attached it to his carriage. Now he knew the exact distance between towns. Within four years the postal service made a profit for the first time ever.

Between 1754 and 1763, Ben traveled to all of the colonies. He sometimes asked Deborah to accompany him. She preferred to stay in Philadelphia. Sally, who was almost twenty, went with her father instead. In 1763, the pair journeyed

Sarah Franklin was born in 1743. Ben nicknamed her Sally.

throughout New England. They met family and friends along the way. They enjoyed the time together.

Ben traveled 1,600 miles that year. Having visited each of the thirteen colonies, Ben Franklin knew America and Americans better than anyone else alive. Although Franklin was not aware of it, he was establishing an important link between the colonies. He connected the scattered colonies through reliable mail service. He created the network by which information could travel quickly. This was important to the colonists before and during the American Revolution.

Benjamin Franklin had come a long way from his boyhood in Boston.

While Ben had been experimenting, he had also been busy in other areas of his life. He wrote many letters to family and friends. He worked on improvements to Philadelphia. The people of Philadelphia elected Ben to represent them in the Pennsylvania Assembly. There he helped run the colony's affairs.

Ben also worked to solve one major problem. Pennsylvania needed protection from enemy attacks. So, a tax was collected to raise money for an armed militia. Everyone paid except Thomas and Richard Penn. Why? Their father had founded Pennsylvania. They felt they should not have to pay taxes to protect their own colony. Only the colonists should have to pay.

Pennsylvania was different from the other twelve colonies because it was owned by the Penns. William Penn had received Pennsylvania from King Charles II of England. The king used the land to pay a debt he owed the Penns. The Penn brothers claimed rights and powers unknown in other colonies. Pennsylvanians were upset that the Penns did not even reside in their colony. They lived in luxury in England.

Ben disagreed with the Penns. So did many other people. In 1757, seeking to right this wrong, Pennsylvania sent Ben to London. He was to meet with the British government and force the Penns to pay their fair share of the tax.

So now, at age fifty-one, Benjamin Franklin crossed the Atlantic Ocean again. This time his son William went with him. Deborah, fearful of sailing, stayed at home with Sally. No one knew that Ben would be gone for five years.

CHAPTER 8

AGENT

BEN AND WILLIAM RENTED LODGING from a Mrs. Stevenson and her daughter Polly in London. Their home was at 7 Craven Street. William began his studies in law. Ben worked as an agent for the Pennsylvania Assembly.

Ben met with immediate frustration. He could not march right into Parliament, England's governing body. Pennsylvania did not have elected officials to represent its colonists in Parliament. Instead, Ben had to convince people little by little of the value of Pennsylvania's complaint against the Penns.

The Penn brothers had many wealthy friends who had great influence in Parliament. Against them, Ben would have to use his wit, wisdom, and patience.

Ben had no real power over the political decisions affecting Pennsylvania. The English Parliament believed they controlled the colonies. The members of Parliament agreed that the Penn brothers were the masters of Pennsylvania.

The Penns met Ben Franklin only once. Angered by Pennsylvania's demands, they refused to see him again. They thought Ben was a pest.

But Ben did not give up. Slowly, he gained an audience for his views. He talked with important people. He shared his ideas with friends. He published information in London papers.

This approach took a long time. However, this left Ben with the chance to enjoy London again. More than thirty years had passed since he had left London as a young man in 1726. Ben was no longer penniless. His electrical experiments had made him famous.

Ben frequently went to the theater. He toured England and Scotland with William. They visited

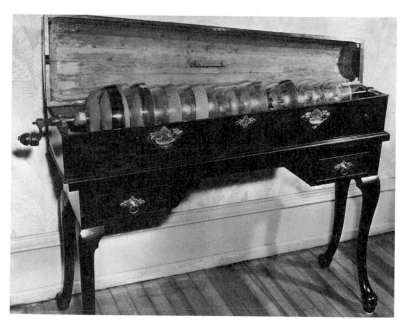

Ben's glass armonica sounded like a stringed instrument when it was played.

Franklin relatives who still lived in the village of Ecton, where Ben's father had grown up. Ben also continued his scientific experiments. Every morning he wrote letters to friends, family, and fellow scientists.

While in England, Ben learned how to play the violin, guitar, and harp. He also invented the "armonica." This musical instrument was made of spinning glass bowls that made delicate music. The glass armonica quickly became popular. Mozart and Beethoven even wrote music for it!

Ben traveled to Edinburgh, Scotland. There he was given another university degree, Doctor of Law. The boy from Boston was now Dr. Benjamin Franklin.

Still, Ben persisted in pressing Pennsylvania's demands. Finally, he persuaded the English government to force the Penns to pay their fair share of taxes. Ben had succeeded in his mission. He also began to understand that the relationship between England and its colonies had grown uneasy. For now, however, he was an Englishman first and an American second. Later, this would change.

On September 4, 1762, Ben's son William married Elizabeth Downes, a wealthy young English woman. Five days later, thirty-one-year-old William was appointed governor of New Jersey. This was a very powerful position for a person his age.

His mission finished, Ben returned home in 1762.

DEFENDER

"ON THE 1ST OF NOVEMBER [1762], I arrived safe and well at my own home...found my wife and daughter well." Much to Ben's delight, Sally had grown into a young woman "with many amicable accomplishments acquired during my absence."

Ben, humble as always, had secretly slipped into Philadelphia. He wanted to avoid any outpouring of welcome. As soon as his friends heard of his return, they came to visit. "My friends were as hearty and affectionate as ever."

In February 1763, William and his wife Elizabeth arrived in America. Ben was pleased to see them. They would live seventeen miles away and he could frequently visit them.

Ben was pleased to return to his wife. Deborah Read Franklin was an affectionate wife but not a good speller. She signed her letters to Ben "your afeckshonet wife."

Ben was almost sixty years old. He looked forward to a restful time now. He would continue working in the Pennsylvania Assembly because he had been reelected each year while he was in England. Ben would also oversee the postal system. He probably thought there would be plenty of time for friends and family. But just as his lightning rod attracted electricity, Ben attracted responsibilities.

Tensions between settlers on the Pennsylvania frontier and Native Americans had grown. Pontiac, a powerful Native American leader, led an uprising against the English colonists. The Native Americans were fighting to keep their homelands.

In 1763, a group of Native Americans was murdered by a mob of colonists. Ben Franklin was angry at the mob's behavior. He felt that the colonists should be grateful for the help that the Native Americans gave to the first settlers. Ben wrote, "These poor People [Native Americans] have always been our Friends. Their Fathers received ours when Strangers here, with Kindness and Hospitality. Behold the Return we have made them!"

Franklin organized an armed militia to confront the mob. Seeing the strength of the militia, the mob gave up and left.

With such unrest at home, Ben began to long for England. He wrote a letter to Polly Stevenson (his English landlady's daughter) in 1763. "Of all the enviable things England has, I envy it most its people," he said.

Although Ben's trip to London had been a success, the Penn brothers still held great power over Pennsylvania. This upset many Pennsylvanians. Ben worked in the Pennsylvania Assembly to lessen the Penns' power. He wanted the Pennsylvania Colony to belong to the King of England rather than to the Penns. Franklin wrote a petition to ask King George III to take control of Pennsylvania. The Assembly adopted his petition.

Who should carry the petition to London? Ben Franklin, of course.

DIPLOMAT

BEN WAS DELIGHTED TO RETURN TO England. In November 1764, he again crossed the Atlantic Ocean. Hundreds of friends watched him leave while cannons roared to signal his departure. When the people of Philadelphia learned he had safely reached London, bells throughout the city rang in Franklin's honor.

Sally had hoped to accompany her father on this trip. But he told her to stay home, take care of her mother, and work on her studies.

By early December 1764, Ben was back in his comfortable lodgings in Mrs. Stevenson's home at 7 Craven Street. Ben found the English people had changed little. However, the English attitude toward the colonies had. The incredible expenses of the French and Indian War had still not been paid. It was very costly to maintain a powerful army and navy to protect the colonies. Someone had to pay these expenses. The English government decided the colonies should pay their fair share. After all, Parliament reasoned, didn't the colonies benefit from the peaceful times?

In 1764, Parliament passed a tax on sugar, coffee, and wines imported from England to America. In 1765, Parliament passed a tax on newspapers, magazines, and playing cards. Dice, wills, almanacs, and marriage licenses were also taxed. Each item needed a stamp to be paid by the purchaser. This tax was called the Stamp Act.

Ben felt this tax was unfair. He worked hard to change it. But he was not a member of Parliament. He had no power.

No one, not even Ben, could have predicted the colonies' response to the Stamp Act. The colonists were outraged to be taxed. After all, they had no representatives to defend them in Parliament. Also, the colonists were used to making decisions for themselves. They were angered that Parliament was now making decisions for them. The colonists threatened the officers who collected the taxes. Some of the officials were attacked. Others had their homes burned. Americans refused to buy the stamps. They refused to buy anything made in England.

Ben's political enemies in Pennsylvania spread rumors about him. They said he was secretly in favor of the Stamp Act so he could make money from it. They said he wanted to be made governor of Pennsylvania. An angry mob threatened Deborah Franklin in her home. Standing on her doorstep, armed with a gun, she turned the mob away.

Ben worked tirelessly to end the Stamp Act. He wrote newspaper articles against it. He persuaded his English friends to help him. In 1766, he was finally asked to appear before Parliament. He had to explain why the colonies were against the Stamp Act.

For four hours, Ben answered 174 questions in the

Some colonists, like these New Yorkers, held public protests against the Stamp Act.

House of Commons. He presented the case for ending the Stamp Act. He used his logic, wit, intelligence, and charm. Franklin won and the

Stamp Act was repealed. But Parliament still claimed the right to make any colonial laws they wished.

Ben Franklin was again a hero in his homeland. However, it was not all work for Ben in London. He found time to travel in both Britain and Europe. He met King Louis XV of France. He conducted experiments and dined with his admirers. He also began his *Autobiography*.

Realizing Franklin's value in England, other American colonies asked him to be their agents. While he was in England, he represented New Jersey, Georgia, Massachusetts, and Pennsylvania.

While he was in London, Ben received news about his family. His beloved daughter Sally married Richard Bache, a merchant. Sadly, Deborah suffered a mild stroke. Ben's sister, Jane Mecom, moved in with Deborah to help. Meanwhile, Deborah watched over the building of a new, larger home on Market Street.

In 1767, under the control of King George III, Parliament passed the Townshend Acts. These new acts taxed tea, glass, and paper imported into America. The colonies revolted. English goods were again boycotted. Parliament repealed most of the taxes in 1770. Only the tax on tea remained. Its purpose was to remind the colonies that England still had the right to tax Americans.

For the next three years little happened between England and America. Franklin knew that unless things changed, however, the colonies might seek independence. Franklin believed England and the colonies could remain together.

But the issue of the tea tax still angered the colonists. From Georgia to Massachusetts, English tea was turned away and sent back to England. The situation exploded in Boston in December of 1773. A group of Bostonians boarded three tea ships. They dumped the tea into the harbor. This event was named the Boston Tea Party. Franklin felt the Boston Tea Party was a mistake. He called it "an act of violent injustice."

Now the English were furious. They got angry

A crowd gathers at Griffin's Wharf in Boston. They watch as 150 men and boys disguised as Native Americans dump tea into Boston Harbor.

with Ben because he represented the colonies. He was blamed for the Boston Tea Party. Ben was called before the Privy Council, a group of the king's advisors. Without saying a word, Franklin calmly endured the harsh words aimed at him as an enemy of England.

Ben knew his time in England was at an end.

To punish the colonists of Boston, the English sent an army to take over the city. This was too

Ben appeared before the Privy Council at Whitehall Chapel in London in 1774.

much for the Americans. The first Continental Congress met in Philadelphia to find ways the colonies could aid Boston.

On April 19, 1775, British troops marched to Lexington, Massachusetts. A battle was fought between British soldiers and American colonists on Lexington Green. The British won and marched further to Concord. There, the colonists stood firm.

They defeated the British, and forced them to retreat to Boston.

The American Revolution had begun. Franklin prepared to leave England. He had many enemies in London now. Old friends turned against him because he supported the colonies. There was even talk he might be put in prison.

In March 1775, Ben sadly sailed back to Philadelphia. He no longer considered himself an Englishman. On the journey he wrote, "It seems that I am too much an American."

When he reached home on May 5, 1775, he found himself a hero and the colonies united against England. He was sixty-nine years old, tired, and sick with gout (an ailment of the legs). During his absence, Deborah had died. Sally and her family moved into Ben's house to be with him. He longed for peace and quiet in his new home. Instead, he was thrust right into the revolution.

REVOLUTIONARY

BEN HAD BEEN HOME LESS THAN A week when he was chosen to represent Pennsylvania in the Second Continental Congress. The Congress met in Philadelphia on May 10, 1775. The delegates were to plan the future of the colonies. Would they remain colonies and compromise with England? Or would they call for independence from England and form a new nation?

In August 1775, King George III declared the colonies in rebellion.

Ben now turned away from his son William, governor of New Jersey. William chose to remain loyal to England. He was captured and put in prison. Ben had the power to help him. But he felt that William was now his enemy. William stayed in prison for the entire war. The break between father and son lasted for the rest of Ben's life.

In the spring of 1776, Franklin went north to ask the people of Canada to join the rebellion. However, Ben could not convince the Canadians to break with England.

Back in Philadelphia, the majority of the delegates now favored American independence from England. On June 24, 1776, a committee was formed to draft a declaration of independence. Thomas Jefferson, John Adams, and Benjamin Franklin were given this duty. Jefferson took on the main writing responsibility. Adams and Franklin added and changed only a few words. On July 1, 1776, the declaration was presented to Congress. But four colonies turned it down.

Ben and others convinced the opposing delegates that independence was necessary. On July 4, 1776, the "Declaration of Independence" was adopted. It was officially signed on August 2, 1776. Knowing the seriousness of their decision, Ben Franklin said,

Ben Franklin signs the Declaration of Independence. The document declares that the American colonies "ought to be Free and Independent States."

"Gentlemen, we must now all hang together, or we shall most assuredly hang separately."

The colonies had declared their right to create a new nation. Now they had to defeat the most powerful army and navy on Earth to form that nation. Ben Franklin's many talents were needed again.

AMBASSADOR

B EN, AT SEVENTY, WAS FAR TOO OLD to carry a gun. His reputation and political skills became his weapons. Congress sent Franklin to France. He was to ask the French for help in the war against England. Ben, Thomas Jefferson, and Silas Deane wanted the French to loan money and ships to the colonies.

France wanted revenge against England for its losses during the French and Indian War. But the French government would not openly join in the American Revolution. Instead, the French secretly sent men and supplies to aid the Americans.

Ben was wildly popular with the French people.

The French had long enjoyed his wit in *Poor Richard's Almanack*. His electrical experiments had made him famous all over France. He was invited to dinners, parties, and balls. In a time when men wore wigs, Ben wore a coonskin cap. This made him look like an American frontiersman. Soon rings, snuff boxes, plates, and medallions carried his famous portrait. In a letter to his daughter Sally, he wrote that his face was "as well known as that of the moon."

Decisions in France were made by the king and his ministers. Ben had to convince them to enter the war openly on the American side. As he wrote, "All of Europe is on our side of the question, as far as applause and good wishes can carry them. We are fighting for their liberty in defending our own." But words and applause could not make bullets or feed an army.

At first the war went poorly for the Americans. General George Washington fought as well as he could. Too often there were not enough guns, food, clothing, or ammunition. Whenever Washington faced the English army, he was defeated.

Ben appears before Queen Marie Antoinette and King Louis XVI (seated) at the Court of France. The queen's companion, Madame Campan, places a crown of laurels on Franklin's head.

The French were worried the Americans would lose the war. So, they remained out of the conflict. Then, in 1777, the Americans won a stunning victory at Saratoga, New York. Over 5,000 British soldiers surrendered.

France took a chance. The king agreed to side with the Americans, and send men, ships, supplies, and money. On February 6, 1778, Ben Franklin signed a treaty with France. The French now recognized the United States as an independent nation.

Ben stayed in France. He worked to make certain that the men and supplies reached America. He was particularly proud when the French ship *The Bonhomme Richard* (named after his character Poor Richard), won a fierce battle with an English warship.

In 1781, at Yorktown, Virginia, Lord Cornwallis surrendered his English army. The success at Yorktown assured American victory and independence.

Ben still had a role to play. He now had to work out a peace treaty between England and the United States. Two years later, in 1783, Benjamin Franklin, representing the new nation, signed the Treaty of Paris. This treaty officially ended the war.

In a letter to a friend he wrote, "We are now friends with England and with all mankind. May we never see another war! For in my opinion there never was a good war or a bad peace."

To another friend he wrote, "America will, with God's blessing, become a great and happy country."

Ben was seventy-seven years old. He was in no hurry to return home. He enjoyed his life in France. He stayed to meet friends and fellow scientists, and to work on his autobiography. He traveled a great deal.

One day, while reading a book in his carriage, he became frustrated. Every time he looked up from his book at the scenery, he had to take off his reading glasses. Then he had to put on another pair so he could see things far away. He thought, why not combine the two lenses? He did and invented bifocal glasses.

Still Ben stayed in France. He wrote, "I am here among a people that love and respect me . . . Perhaps I may . . . die among them." He felt far removed from America. "I have been so long abroad that I should now be almost a stranger in my own country."

A crowd of well-wishers greets Ben upon his return to Philadelphia.

But in 1785, Ben decided to return to the United States. Seeking peace and quiet, he went home to Philadelphia. He found just the opposite. "We landed at Market Street, where we were received by a crowd of [cheering] people. Found my family well. God be praised and thanked for all his mercies!" Church bells rang out his welcome. For an entire week he had a stream of guests.

Ben barely had time to settle in before he was called upon by his countrymen once again. He was made president of Pennsylvania. As the state's chief official, he worked on matters pertaining to Pennsylvania and its people.

The new nation called upon his talents, too. The American Revolution had been won. The United States was now an independent nation. But what kind of government would the new country have? Certainly, wise old Benjamin Franklin would have some advice and ideas.

He did.

REPRESENTATIVE

THE THIRTEEN COLONIES HAD worked together successfully to win the war. Now the war was over and their independence was guaranteed. Could they still cooperate under one government?

In 1787, Ben was named as a delegate to the Constitutional Convention to help create that government. George Washington was the convention's president. Fortunately for Ben, the convention met down the street from his home in Philadelphia. Walking was difficult for him now. He had to be carried to the meetings.

The convention had fifty-five delegates from the thirteen states. Franklin was the oldest. There was much arguing and heated discussion. Ben listened to the discussions and made suggestions. Franklin believed that if each side would give a little, together they could create a government for all.

The small states felt the larger states had too much power. The states with larger populations thought they should have more power because they had more people. Ben proposed two lawmaking houses. The Senate would have two senators from each state, no matter the size of its population. In the House of Representatives the states with more people would have more representatives.

This compromise gave the United States the two houses of Congress we have today.

Ben was forced to make a compromise himself, one which he did not like. He wanted to end slavery, but over half the delegates owned slaves. Franklin felt he could not push for an end to slavery at the time. First, he needed to help build a country governed by laws.

The final draft of the Constitution was presented.

George Washington presided over the Constitutional Convention at the Pennsylvania State House in Philadelphia. It lasted from May 25, 1787, to Sept. 17, 1787.

Ben felt it should be adopted unanimously. He wrote, "Mr. President,...I consent, sir, to this Constitution, because I expect no better, and because I am not sure that it is not the best."

Ben made one last comment during the convention. Carved on the back of George Washington's chair was a sun with rays bursting out from it. Franklin had gazed at that sun during the convention. After the Constitution was signed, he said, "I did not know if the sun was rising or setting. Now I know it is a rising sun."

Eventually, all thirteen states ratified the Constitution. It became the law of the land on March 4, 1789. On April 30, 1789, George Washington was sworn in as the first president of the United States.

Benjamin Franklin was the only one of the founding fathers to sign all four documents creating the United States: the Declaration of Independence, the treaty with France, the peace treaty with England, and the Constitution. This was quite a remarkable accomplishment for a boy from Boston.

CHAPTER 14

BENJAMIN FRANKLIN REMEMBERED

BEN SPENT HIS LAST FEW YEARS with his friends and family. He enjoyed the company of his grandchildren. Every day he helped his nine-year-old granddaughter Deborah with her spelling lessons.

Ben read, talked, advised, wrote, and thought. He even worked hard to have the turkey named as the national symbol of America. He wrote, "The turkey is a much more respectable bird [than the eagle]...a true original native of America."

Ever mindful of doing public good, in 1790, he asked Congress to end slavery.

Ben's life was long and full. Born the son of a

Boston candle-maker, he grew up to be wealthy and world famous. But age caught up with him. The last year of his life was painful. He suffered from kidney stones. He was often bedridden and lost his appetite.

Always cheerful, even on his deathbed, he wrote a letter to a friend. He said he would die with "little Regret, as, having seen during a long life a good deal of this world, I feel a growing curiosity to be acquainted with some other."

On April 17, 1790, at age eighty-four, Benjamin Franklin died peacefully in his home. With him were his family, his books, and his inventions. As he had wished, Ben was buried beside his wife Deborah in Christ Church Burial Ground in Philadelphia. Nearby was the grave of his beloved son Francis.

To honor Benjamin Franklin, Congress declared thirty days of mourning throughout America. Over 20,000 people attended Franklin's funeral. This was the largest crowd ever to gather in Philadelphia. Bells tolled. Flags flew at half-staff. *The Pennsylvania Gazette*, issue number 3125, was printed with black borders, telling of Ben's death.

Benjamin and Deborah Franklin are buried in the cemetery of Christ Church in Philadelphia. Visitors often throw a penny on their grave for good luck.

When he was much younger, Ben thought he would be most remembered as a printer. He had jokingly written these words for his headstone:

The Body of
B. Franklin Printer,
(Like the Cover of an old Book
Its Contents torn out
And stript of its Lettering & Gilding)
Lies here, Food for Worms.
But the Work shall not be lost;
For it will (as he believ'd) appear once more
In a new and more elegant Edition
Revised and corrected,
By the Author.

Ben was much more than a printer, however. He was a father, an inventor, a scientist, a diplomat, an author, a husband, a friend, and an American.

Even without all the writing Ben Franklin left, the world would still remember his remarkable life. His legacy includes fire departments, a national postal system, free libraries, a hospital, and a university. His inventions from bifocal glasses to lightning rods make life easier and safer for people.

Epitaph written 1728.

The Body of
B Franklin Printer,
(Like the Cover of an old Book
Its Contents torn out
And stript of its Lettering & Gilding)
Lies here, Food for Worms.
But the Work shall not be lost;
For it will, (as he believ'd) appear once more,
In a new and more elegant Edition
Revised and corrected,
By the Author.

Ben Franklin's epitaph in his own handwriting

Franklin is also remembered in names across the land. Hundreds of cities, towns, townships, and counties are named Franklin. Tennessee was almost named Franklin in his honor. Mountains and lakes have been named for the man who tamed lightning and help found a nation.

Benjamin Franklin, born without privilege or wealth, rose through hard work, intelligence, and determination to become one of the most influential people of his century or any other.

CHRONOLOGY

1706	(January 17) Ben Franklin is born in Boston, Massachusetts Colony.
1718	Becomes printer's apprentice to James, his older brother.
1722	Writes his Silence Dogood essays that are published anonymously in his brother's newspaper, *The New England Courant*.
1723	Runs away to Philadelphia where he works as a printer.
1724–26	Lives and works as a printer in London. Returns to Philadelphia to clerk in a store.
1727	Founds the Junto.
1728	Opens print shop with partner Hugh Meredith.
1729	Purchases *The Pennsylvania Gazette* newspaper.
1730	Marries Deborah Read.
1732	Publishes *Poor Richard's Almanack*.
1736–37	Founds Union Fire Company and is appointed postmaster of Philadelphia.
1742–44	Founds the University of Pennsylvania, and invents the Franklin stove.
1751	Publishes his work on electricity, founds Pennsylvania Hospital, and is elected to the Pennsylvania Assembly.
1752	Performs kite experiment with son William and invents lightning rods to protect buildings.

1753	Awarded the Copley Medal from the Royal Society for his electrical experiments.
1753–54	Appointed Deputy Postmaster General for all of the American Colonies.
1757	Sails to England as a representative of the Pennsylvania Assembly.
1762	Returns to Philadelphia.
1764–75	Lives in London, and works for repeal of Stamp Act.
1775	Speaks before England's House of Commons on the Stamp Act. Returns to Philadelphia and is elected to the Continental Congress.
1776	Signs the Declaration of Independence. Sails to France to gain French help for the United States.
1778	Signs Treaty of Alliance with France.
1783	Negotiates peace treaty with Britain to end the American Revolution.
1785	Returns to America.
1787	Becomes a delegate to the Constitutional Convention. Signs the Constitution.
1790	(April 17) Dies in Philadelphia; buried in Christ Church Burial Ground.

BIBLIOGRAPHY

Donovan, Frank R. *The Many Worlds of Benjamin Franklin*. New York: American Heritage, 1963.

Franklin, Benjamin. *Autobiography*. Boston: Houghton Mifflin & Co., 1896.

————. *Poor Richard's Almanack*. Mount Vernon, New York: Peter Pauper Press, 1995.

Judson, Clara. *Benjamin Franklin*. Chicago: Follett Publishing Co., 1957.

Lopez, Claude-Anne. *Benjamin Franklin's "Good House."* Washington, D.C.: Division of Publications, National Park Service, 1981.

Rogers, George L., editor. *Benjamin Franklin's The Art of Virtue: His Formula For Successful Living*. Eden Prairie, Minnesota: Acorn Publishing, 1996.

Tunis, Edwin. *Colonial Living*. New York: Thomas Y. Crowell, 1957.

Van Doren, Carl. *Benjamin Franklin*. New York: The Viking Press, 1938.

Wright, Esmond, editor. *Benjamin Franklin: His Life as He Wrote It*. Cambridge, Massachusetts: Harvard University Press, 1989.

FURTHER READING

Cobblestone Magazine. Volume Thirteen, Number Seven, September, 1992. (The entire issue is about Benjamin Franklin.)

Davidson, Margaret. *The Story of Benjamin Franklin, Amazing American.* New York: Dell, 1988.

Fritz, Jean. *What's the Big Idea, Benjamin Franklin?* New York: Putnam, 1976.

Giblin, James Cross. *The Amazing Life of Benjamin Franklin.* New York: Scholastic, 2000.

Lawson, Robert. *Ben and Me.* Boston: Little, Brown, 1988.

FOR MORE INFORMATION

Benjamin Franklin: An Enlightened American
This Web site contains information about all aspects of Ben's life, everything from examples of his wit and humor to explanations of his discoveries and inventions. This site also includes the Franklin family tree.

Web site: library.thinkquest.org/22254/home.htm

Benjamin Franklin National Memorial
This memorial is located at the Franklin Institute Science Museum in Philadelphia, Pennsylvania. Both Memorial Hall and a 20-foot-high statue of Benjamin Franklin remind people of Franklin's contributions to the United States of America. Some of Ben's original possessions, such as his armonica and odometer, are on display in Memorial Hall.

Web site: www.fi.edu/tfi/exhibits/memorial.html

Benjamin Franklin's Autobiography
This Web site contains the entire text of Benjamin Franklin's *Autobiography*. It also includes essays written by Franklin and a time line of his life.

Web site: odur.let.rug.nl/~usa/B/bfranklin/frankxx.htm

The Franklin Institute Science Museum
Visitors to the museum's Web site can explore a section called "Benjamin Franklin: Glimpses of the Man." It contains information about Benjamin Franklin's role in politics and science. The museum's goal is to continue Benjamin Franklin's dedication to helping the public understand science.
(222 North 20 Street, Philadelphia, PA 19103)
Phone: (215) 448-1200

Web site: www.fi.edu/franklin

The Library Company of Philadelphia
With the support of the Junto, Benjamin Franklin founded The Library Company of Philadelphia in 1731. The Library contains books, prints, and photographs that help people understand what America was like from its founding days to the end of the 1800s. (1314 Locust Street, Philadelphia, PA 19107)
Phone: (215) 546-3181

Web site: www.librarycompany.org/homepage.htm

Poor Richard's Web Site
Benjamin Franklin is well known for the sayings he wrote and included in *Poor Richard's Almanack*. This Web site includes many of Franklin's most famous sayings.

Web site: www.crosswinds.net/~poorrichard

PHOTO CREDITS

Library of Congress (Washington, DC):
  9 (LC# D418-50297),
  15,
  27 (LC# D418-28053),
  29 (LC# D419-170),
  49,
  52 (LC# D416-28058),
  67 (LC# D419-175),
  88,
  93 (LC# D416-28056),
  97,
  100 (LC# D416-28055);

North Wind Picture Archives (Alfred, ME): 17, 40, 44, 84, 105, 111;

Library Company of Philadelphia (Philadelphia, PA): 21;

Brown Brothers (Sterling, PA): 31, 37, 54, 65, 87, 109;

The Franklin Institute (Philadelphia, PA): 61, 75;

Culver Pictures (New York, NY): 70, 78

INDEX

Bold numbers refer to photographs

ABOUT THE AUTHORS

Since 1980, Peter and Connie Roop have written sixty fiction and nonfiction books for young readers. They have written biographies, nature books, historical fiction, and have edited the actual journals of the Pilgrims, Lewis and Clark, and Columbus.

The Roops enjoy writing the stories they find in history. Through research and imagination, they have experienced a Blackfeet buffalo jump in Montana and sailed with Columbus. They have followed the footsteps of Benjamin Franklin in Philadelphia and spied for George Washington. They have kept lighthouse lights burning and searched for whales. Through learning about history, the Roops hope to share the stories of people who lived long ago with the readers of today.

Connie teaches high-school environmental science. At her school, she has grown a prairie and dug a wetland. Peter, now a full-time author and speaker, taught elementary school for twenty-five years. He was named Wisconsin State Teacher of the Year in 1987.

When not writing or teaching, the Roops travel with their children, Heidi and Sterling. Their goal as a family is to travel to all seven continents together. So far, they have visited South America, North America, and Europe. Africa is next!